PRAISE FOR *AN AFF*~~~~ ~~~~

In these finely crafted and tantalizing poems, Steve Trenam returns us to that soul-intersection where the human art of being—the performance of living, the pure human consummation of it—achieves a pinnacle of release and affirmation. Those moments when we spread our spiritual wings and ascend, buoyant against the mortal coil, before shambling off into the inevitable dust. Aptly titled, *An Affront to Gravity* is a derogation of those realities that seemingly hold us down, hold us back, condemn us all. A skipped rock will ultimately sink, admits the poet—but not before sending shivering ripples across the surface of a pond. Feeding apples to stallions in the Tuscan Hills, our worldly circumstances are transfigured. In this mortal world, gravity may hold the ultimate card. But in the interim, and in our junctures of great unheralded glory, we may not just forestall the weight of mortality, but commute its sentence entirely. Gravity loses its full dominion over few of us entirely—but there are rare meridians of small majesty, however temporary, for us all—moments when we may blow our jazz so hard we blow the leaves off trees; that remain as suspended in memory and as perfectly turned as an egg on a thin, wide, stainless steel blade. That's no small triumph of being, and it is a delight to experience, however vicariously. These are poems that hold us spellbound in an ecstasy of pendulous light.
—George Wallace is Writer in Residence at the Walt Whitman Birthplace, first poet laureate of Suffolk County, LI NY and author of 36 books and chapbooks of poetry.

In this remarkable collection, Trenam is able to transform empty and blank spaces into places of worship that entice the reader to leave "the dark corners of our rooms" to experience not only the world that he creates through these poems, but also the ways in which art, music, dance, and poetry are rooted "at the heart of things." Just as he speaks of Cezanne, how "his art moves us ahead of ourselves—/out of bounds, transcending our limits" so do the lines and scenes in this unique collection, where images loom and dance, at once recognizing the history from which they are speaking, the gravity that sustains those boundaries, and the way that expression, in every form, can stretch and alter them. As the initial poem, "Full Circle" suggests, the reader will want to return to these pages again and again, meeting different versions of themselves, but also knowing that both the questions these poems elicit and the beauty they curate have no real end.

—Megan Merchant, author of "*Before the Fevered Snow*" (Stillhouse Press, 2020). She was awarded the 2016-2017 COG Literary Award, the 2018 Beullah Rose Poetry Prize, and most recently, second place in the Pablo Neruda Prize for Poetry. She is an editor at *Pirene's Fountain* and *The Comstock Review.*

Hold tight to your kite strings… it's liftoff! Look, there's "Stravinsky's bird on fire," here's "Christo's running fence—a choreographed fugue." Steve Trenam is a gravity-defying word-dancer who rambles, romps, canters, and glissades his stories and images into our hearts. He punctuates these flights of fancy with delightfully quirky humor, offering up a unique stew of associations with nods to the Book of Revelation, IHOP, haystacks without needles, clouds behind silver linings, and Kurosawa's unrelenting rain. But in their exuberant flight, these poems also offer unflinching, clear gazes into the difficult—deaths of brothers and friends, glimpses of our own mortality.

From "poppy seeds winging their way to burst into air" to "exalted splashes of color" *affronts to gravity* abound in this collection. But perhaps Trenam's most powerful affront is his defiant celebration of our inevitable landing. With the spirit of a dancer ("proud of his lunacy") he praises "the thrill of falling" and assures us, "Downhill is going to be fun."

—Prartho Sereno, Poet Laureate Emerita of Marin County, author of 4 prize-winning poetry collections, most recently *Indian Rope Trick*

An Affront to Gravity

Poems and Salutations

Steve Trenam

BLUE LIGHT PRESS
1st WORLD
PUBLISHING

San Francisco | Fairfield | Delhi

An Affront to Gravity

Steve Trenam

ISBN: 978-1-4218-3675-1

Library of Congress Control Number: 2020946630

Cover photograph: "Moon Over Nicasio Reservoir," by Jeffrey Bartfeld.
Cover design by Jeffrey Bartfeld, Ellie Portner, and Steve Trenam.

1ST WORLD LIBRARY
PO Box 2211
Fairfield, Iowa 52556
www.1stworldpublishing.com

BLUE LIGHT PRESS
www.bluelightpress.com
Email: bluelightpress@aol.com

ACKNOWLEDGEMENTS

My gratitude goes out to Diane Frank for getting me off my duff and into print, and particularly for her Book Angel campaign on my behalf. I can't tell you how moved I am by the support I've received from the talented authors under Diane's broad wings. It also goes to Prartho Sereno for her unrivaled voice and the wisdom of her workshops, and for Ada Limon, simply because she is a star in the firmament who will only settle for "the big bite, one restless, tooth-filled mouth to take me down."

I wish to thank my daughter, Eliana, for her unwavering support as an editor, and for her passion in the pursuit of her art form—her resiliency, her ability to persevere, her steadfast determination to become an accomplished performer. It is the joy she projects from the stage as much as the skill and grace of her dancing that moves me.

Jeffrey Bartfeld took the photograph for the cover, and both Jeffrey and Ellie Portner fashioned a brazen affront to that beatific photo by abusing it mercilessly in Photoshop. Don't ask me how Jeffrey got that nude woman to lie across Nicasio Reservoir in the moonlight. And Jeffrey is also responsible for introducing me to Diane and Prartho, a kindness for which I shall always be grateful.

I also want to express appreciation to my fellow members of Poetic License Sonoma who take liberties to spread poetry everywhere within reach.

And finally, I want to recognize my poetry writing class of the Santa Rosa Junior College Older Adult Program for the savvy flair and joy they bring to our classroom every single week.

For my daughter, Eliana

and in memory of
Alan Sandy
and Bernie Sugarman

CONTENT

Poems

Salutations

"I am greeted each morning
by the sheer weight
of Cezanne's boulders
hanging from my wall,
their rounded enormity held aloft
by a tiny brass hook—
a visual affront to gravity."

— From "A Stone's Throw"

Poems

Full Circle

Hanging on a note
en pointe, just so,
while the Universe hums
O watch her body sway!
My sedentary bones bask in her glow.

Eliana is two and a half.
We hear a screech
and run into the room
where *Swan Lake* is on PBS.
"Are you OK?"

She points to the screen
and exclaims, "That!"
"We can take you to the ballet."
She says, "No! That!"
"You mean you want
to do that, to *be* that."
"Yes! Yes!"

Twenty-seven years later
she is Stravinsky's bird
on fire.

From her perch offstage
she bursts through the air,
landing in a flurry of red,
her arms unfurling into supple,
slowly strumming wings.

Stravinsky's lifeblood flows
through her movement—
notes and dancer so in sync
she becomes the instrument—
sound itself.

Assessing her domain,
the Firebird burns slowly.
With her leg extended
she taps the ground around her,
probing her surroundings.

This is where she belongs—
the Firebird controls her realm.
The dancer dominates the stage—
she is a bird through and through,
a flaming blur across
the toe-bruised floor.

At home with the music,
with her movement,
with the audience,
joyful beyond a young girl's dreams.

Waiting outside the stage door,
a young girl, about four,
in red leotard and tutu
pirouettes in the hall,
holding a single rose,
and as she turns, sings,
"The Bird
        The Bird
                The Bird."

SEAMS

In my truculent youth
I would take my radiant body
outside to steam
against the frigid moonlight
before going back in
to her bed once more.

That road is now taken
by the adolescent jogs
of younger men
and I am off
the beaten path
that rambles on without me.

I no longer seek to shock
the cold night air.
I now slip into the warm embrace
of your comforter
to sample your lovely bones
with a more focused, gentler touch.

You fashion from falling leaves
the autumn fabric of my being.
You do not sew hastily;
you work my ragged, rough-hewn edges
until my seams lie gracefully
over your supple length and breadth.

You are even more inviting
than the bowl of ripe plums
perched on the windowsill
scenting the morning air.
I do my very best
to lead you astray.

My hand goes gently there—
the tips of my fingers chassé
down the small of your back,
over its scar-sewn hollow,
transforming that soft, pliant surface
into an invitation to dance.

ROMPING WITH BEARS

I want to romp with Charlie Musselwhite
and other big blue bears who blow
emotion into the universe.
Sonny Rollins, for instance, who shambles
toward an audience with notes so big
his paws can't hold them.
One needs room to confront such bears.

Maybe an old tavern in Marshall
with the sea lapping at the bar-room floor,
bikers beguiled by Charlie's harmonica.
Perhaps a bridge after midnight will do,
or a smaller New York Five Spot.

At the Russian River Jazz Festival,
Sonny once blew leaves off trees
in June,
stopped all river traffic
and antics on the beach
with the first nine earth-shaking
notes from his tenor sax.
A jazz critic shook his head and said,
"That's why they call him 'The Man.'"

Without their harmonic progressions
above the pull of gravity,
I would expect these behemoths
to be eating berries,
rolling down hills,
and gathering no musical moss.

But when they improvise, they cast
their shadows across the moon,
and on some cloudless nights
we can hear them blow cadences
that runnel through our bones
and Be Bop our blues away.

NIP

When you entered the room,
conversation stopped.
All eyes went to you—
long supple legs moving
with self-assured grace,
an aloof countenance
shielding secret warmth.

When your startling
blue eyes met mine,
they narrowed thoughtfully
and I was smitten.
I had an overwhelming urge
to hold you in my arms.
Knew you were with someone,
but how could you belong
to anyone?

You were self-prepossessed
and free.

I approached you,
said come away with me.
You did not object.

Most of the guests had left.
Your companion
was in another room.
I whisked you out
the front door
and into my car.

You were quiet as I drove home,
seemed to be taken
with streetlights as they passed.
I wondered about your name,
and what late-night treat
I might offer you.

Maybe 7-Eleven
will have some cat food.

A Stone's Throw
Porcelain Bowl
7 X 16 inches.

A Stone's Throw

I am greeted each morning
by the sheer weight
of Cezanne's boulders
hanging from my wall,
their rounded enormity held aloft
by a tiny brass hook—
a visual affront to gravity.

Cezanne bends perception,
echoes our need to experience
things differently.
His art moves us ahead of ourselves--
out of bounds, transcending our limits.

Cezanne's boulders send ripples
beyond the pond,
exceeding our grasp.
My stone barely skims the surface.
I need a bigger rock.

My living room wall
will not support their weight,
yet there they hang,
expanding my reality
into its own informed expression.
I will keep tossing my stones,
and I will watch the ripples grow

deeper and wider with each throw.

ABOVE IT ALL

after Prartho Sereno

If a certain bird
flies high enough,
gravity loses its dominion
and she just glides
in the somnambulant air,
above everything—
never having
to clutch a branch
or touch the earth
again.

She becomes a buoy floating
in a stratospheric sea,
denying the pull of the moon
with a solitary serenity.

Her only major concern—
What will she do
with the eggs?

WHITE

A solitary black bird
perches atop a wooden gate
at the far left of a snow-covered fence
keeping pace with a country road.
Tracks of a shadowy horse,
for the moment, a phantom,
form a spellbinding contrast
to the white surround.

I say white as if it were
readily identifiable in its purity,
but the white in the shade
along the base of the fence
is blue,
and the whites at the tips of the trees
around the house blush slightly
in the fading sunlight.

A certain slant of light
clings to the snow-crowned roof
and a veil of sullen white
looms above the horizon.
An illusory white cloak
obscures the horse's back,
and the fence is capped with whites,
running rampant through the shadows.

In point of fact,
seventy-six shades of white exist
in this one painting alone—
Monet's *Magpie*.
By his own admission,
the most significant challenge
ever to face the end
of his youthful brush,

with or without a horse.

THE MUSCULARITY OF RISK

I'd like to experience the thrill of falling,
not the unobserved tragedy of Bruegel's Icarus,
but with applause for a soft landing.
No waxen legs going down for a third time,
but legs galumphing up onto the shore.

And not Webster's galumph,
"to move along heavily and clumsily,"
but Louis Carroll's combination
of gallop and triumph.
Having survived a fall like that,
a triumphant gallop surely must follow.

Unhitch the plow horse and go for a ride.
Dry off under a Tumtum tree
and admire the tulgey wood
as all beamish boys should.

Trot home and flatten your elders
with how far you fell.
They should be proud of your lunacy,
for who among them would have taken the risk?

Bluster on into town
and tell anyone who'll listen,
you are the Cedar Waxwing
of humanity,
an exalted splash of color
to enliven the pulse of poets
everywhere.

BLAME

I was 16, my friend 19,
a lepidopterist. Peaceful
star-lit outings
out D Street Extension—
white sheet on a hillside,
lantern at its center,
moths drawn to the flame.

Thousands labeled
and pinned in shallow drawers,
new species named after him.
All he could want.

I introduced my friend
to my younger brother
but never knew
they saw one another.
I was three years older.
Different schools.
Different buddies.
Not as close
as we might have been.

We remained distant as adults
until his diabetes worsened
thirty years later
and I reached out to him.
We met near Bass Lake
in the Sierras.

We sat on the bank
touching on childhood memories,
not leaping into anything,
our lines limp in the water,
as hesitant as the trout
we were failing to catch.
Something unspoken between us.

It wasn't until the end
of our three-day stay
that he told me
I had put him in harm's way,
ruined his life.

My moth collecting friend
once asked what I thought of
a mutual friend's body.
I had said, "He's an athlete.
So what?"
I tried to visualize my friend
reeling in my brother—
how blind had I been?

"I didn't know. I had no idea."
But he was on his way home—
didn't want to hear
about teenage naiveté.

The next day, a message—
my brother's voice in tears.
He'd come to realize
all the years he'd wasted
blaming me,
and how much it meant
to discover I loved him.

That was the last time I heard his voice.
Denied a new kidney,
operation too risky.
Ate potato salad,
got potassium poisoning,
went into a coma.
Flew down to see him.
Eight doctors treating him—
        [not caring for him]
No one in charge.
He remained unresponsive.
I returned home and waited.

A few days later,
a surgeon called for permission
to slice my brother's penis
to relieve imagined priapism.
I mentioned his wire implant—
surely in his chart.
        [embarrassed pause]
He relayed this to his interns.
I heard one snort and say,
"Moot point, he just died."

I went back down.
Talked to his friends.
They said nice things,
but seemed distant.
Brought his body home.

Tormented by his abusers,
questioning myself,
I buried him.

Preface to "Running Fence"

If you were not around in 1976 when Christo Javacheff created his 24-½ mile fence in Sonoma County, California, then you missed something extraordinary. Historically speaking, it is noteworthy that the Smithsonian Museum has called Christo's *Running Fence* one of the greatest works of art of the twentieth century, and two films have been made about it. It took Christo four years of dealing with local and state governments to get the necessary permits, not to mention convincing fifty-nine landowners, mostly farmers and ranchers who knew little about art, to allow him to erect his fence across their properties. But that was just part of the creative process for Christo—the art of negotiation. In the end, it was as if he had become a member of all their families. In 2009, at the thirty-third anniversary of the *Running Fence*, I watched for hours as he greeted by name, every landowner and worker who approached him. Amazing.

My poem is, in one sense, a reflection of how I experienced the fence, but it is also a celebration of how the artist drew attention, not only to his artwork, but to the gentle contours of the rolling hills the fence so gracefully meandered across.

RUNNING FENCE

Christo Javacheff
and his wife Jeanne-Claude
fabricate a contrapuntal fence,
a choreographed fugue
with Sonoma County's hills.

A smoke and black motorcycle
catches the Running Fence
poised on a hinge of time—
a billowing brief evocation
of the land around it.

As the sun sheds the night,
a startling pink stain
emerges along the bottoms
of shimmering white skirts,
gathering evanescent dew.

The fence and the rider
skim across the countryside,
the engine thrumming beneath
ribbons of their passage
until fog intercedes.

They playfully serpentine
in and out, rising, falling,
rollicking through the mist
leading to, let's just say,
a precipitous plunge into the sea.

The fence is history,
as we will soon enough be,
but these gentle hills abound
waiting for us to leave
the dark corners of our rooms.

NARROW ENDS
(WITH A NOD TO CHARLES WRIGHT)

The narrow end of a wintery afternoon
Where the pallid light
of a day grown old
deigns to suggest:
    "Play the hand you've been dealt."

A blank slate is otherworldly—
An unfilled niche.
It doesn't apply to us:
What is writ is writ.
    Fate holds all the cards.

One and one are still only one—
a solitary number, each of us
measuring time and distance,
each of us out of our depths—
    blades of grass pushing up boulders.

Stepping lightly along
the edge of our discontent,
time only runs out.
No one's there to turn the hourglass
    or dig down to the marrow.

Wayfarer, compose yourself.
Take stock of your hand, yes.
Then talk yourself into something.
Take up the two-step and
dance to the music
    before time and distance stop.

PREFACE TO "A SUMMER DAY"

I heard Mary Oliver's poem, "The Summer Day," read a while back on *The New Yorker Radio Hour* on National Public Radio. It is one of the most popular poems she ever composed. A prayerful poem, beautifully written, but not my experience of Mother Nature! Were I to have knelt or fallen down into Mary's grass, or strolled through her fields, I would have emerged with ticks embedded in my legs, spider bites in tender portions of my anatomy, a smattering of red ants in my shoes, pollen in my sinuses, and an unidentifiable rash I would have been unable to reach to scratch.

And what, pray tell, is she doing feeding a beatific grasshopper sugar out of the palm of her hand? Nature's bounty? I don't think so. It is an insect that, should the practice continue, will soon need an insulin pump.

Please don't regard the following poem as anti-Mary Oliver; I like her poem very much. My version is simply a different look at how Mother Nature really works.

A Summer Day

When I heard a cacophony of crows
outside my door, I stuck my nose out
to see the reason for the ruckus
and found the pine tree
near my cottage
covered in riotous birds,
black with them
all cawing at a commotion
on the ground.

Something was being killed,
and the crows were taking exception;
this in spite of the fact
I had seen a murder of crows
just the day before
chase a squirrel into traffic
to render that morsel tender.

In the middle of my driveway,
a hawk's combative wings
were fighting for ballast
as her talons and beak
gripped and ripped
a once brassy blue jay—
dust and feathers in the air,
blue snow fluttering to the ground.

Her victim lifeless,
Accipiter velox (an apt name for a raptor),
sunk her claws
into the remains of the jay
and with effort, took flight,
slowly carrying her prey
across grass-laden fields
into the distance,
pursued, not too closely,
by a handful of her critics.

As I turned to walk back in,
I came face to face
with a wide, skillfully woven web.
At its core, struggling to free
her pale forearms
and gossamer wings,
Mary Oliver's grasshopper,
soon to be sewn
into a silken shroud—

No sugar in the hand
dealt this summer day.

I had made no attempt
to rescue the jay,
nor do I contrive an intervention
with the imperious spider
aroused from the still edge of waiting.
Instead, I stride into the kitchen,
close the door behind me,
and devour a healthy serving
of ham and eggs
     over

       e

       a

       s

       y

before settling the dust of my years
into the wind-swept threat
of my living room
to be idle and blessed
pondering just what it is
I plan to do
with what's left
of my one wild and precious life.

Sixteen

Years from now,
when I summon up
remembrance of things past,
you will be the garden
at the heart of things,

and when I think of you,
the mistakes I've made
will fade from view.
My life's failures are in
the not having done,

which will not be the case
with you.
You scatter joy randomly
simply by doing
the things you love.

You are an artist
who carries her mastery
of form in her body.
I could watch you dance
forever.

Turning a Corner

for my niece, Bambi

Lightly browned on one side,
she lifts and balances it
sunny side up
on the thin, wide, stainless steel blade.

She suspends it
in the air
feeling the weight of it.

This is not an egg,
it is a fifty-year-old recipe
she is regarding,
reflecting on its ingredients—
the combined look of them.

She decides they are nicely blended
and only half done.
She turns it over in her mind,
once more, hesitating...

In one luxuriant movement
she flips it
to its other side,
then sprinkles more pepper

and says softly to herself,
"Downhill is going to be fun."

GREY MATTER 1

Patches of hair missing.
Bald spots on my chest.
Wires leading to a screen
not yet illuminated.
Bright light above me.
A disembodied voice
tells me to roll onto my left side.
The image suddenly appears.

I am stunned, transfixed, stupefied.
Instantly aware this procedure
would be better performed
in the dark.
          I would much prefer to be lying etherized
             upon the steel of this gauzy table
than watching the pulsating image
of the life within me
laboring to continue.

As the lab tech works the controls,
the object on the screen rotates,
expanding and contracting,
not rhythmically,
but breathing hard.
How long can it do this?
The little red engine,
chugging up the steep incline
of vitality
as if it thought it could.

I feel compelled to watch
as attenuated chambers
propel grey fluid
through loose fitting flaps
with phantom hinges.
        This is such stuff as dreams
        are made of.
I am a mouse in a magnetic field
waiting for an owl.

GREY MATTER 2

Following my echocardiogram,
I envision the formation
of plaque, and clots
insecurely lodged
in small crevices.
I think of my indolence—
hours in an easy chair
watching TV,
eating red meat.

While I wait for the results—
early to bed,
rigorous walks,
a newfound fondness for lettuce,
and visualizing
Billy Collins perennials:
irises, tulips, and peonies
smiling up at me.

Fifteen days
after peering into the void,
a letter arrives
bearing the word "Normal."
I do not read the fine print.
I resume the sanity
of complete denial,
save for this periodic spasm
of memory.

LEAP OF FAITH

I take my daughter to the ballet studio
at a former convent in Marin.
She will be dancing for hours.

At the edge of the church's property
is an old gymnasium.
I ascend the stairs and find the door
unlocked. The gym is empty.
Through a long expanse of windows,
improvisational sunlight flows—
dust particle adagios in the slipstream.
I can almost hear *A Love Supreme*
in the sonorous morning air.

Two small birds enter
through a broken window
and sing their way up
to a nest in the rafters,
riffing on a Coltrane refrain.

I notice a rack of balls
at the far end of the court
and start shooting free throws,
expand to twenty footers,
and finally, the fantasy
of a half-court shot.

Reminded of my distant past
scrimmaging the Warriors—
Rick Barry in his prime
driving the baseline,
gliding like my daughter
as she glissades across her floor—
effortless and magical.

I retire to the stands
to reflect on my spent youth,
my daughter making music visible,
her grand jetés,
higher than I could ever leap,
even in my heyday.

My reflective soul resides
in this dusty relic of a building,
playing court to my form of ballet—
as close as I will ever come
to a place of worship.

ILLUMINATION—A TANKA

Pulsing like fireflies,
the lights in the streets below
clarify the night
and a memory of you
that sparks my body's longing.

LUCE

As the last glint of sunlight
lingered at the edge of darkness,
I was struck by how perfect
my day had been,
and by how much I wanted
it to continue.

Market Day on
the Roman stones of Poppi—
Ivo drawing his knife
through a leg of prosciutto,
handing us bread
drizzled with oil,
sprinkled with salt.

In every village
an incitement of gelato.
Watching my daughter
milk her first cow.
The stream-fed pond
below our villa.
The Tuscan hills
outside our window.
Seeking the wild Hoopah.
Feeding apples to a stallion
and four mares.
The sunset just completed.

As stars expanded,
the sky darkened
and fireflies began
to express themselves,
sweeping low,
brushing the night air
with a pulsating glow—
a persistent intermittence,
a momentary glimpse.

These tiny meandering
bearers of light,
on and off reminders
of the impermanence of pattern:
the fleeting phosphorescence
of this perfect day,
the lightning bug journey
of our unsustainable lives.
Even the unrelenting radiance
of a star.

FRIDAY THE THIRTEENTH

His narrow-brimmed fedora,
a passionless grey,
hung precariously from the bedpost
where he had cavalierly
tossed it the night before.
A mistake—
a hat on the bed was bad luck.

He went downstairs
to irresolutely greet the day.
He wasn't terribly superstitious,
but could it hurt to knock on wood
after saying something risky
like "fine" or "wonderful?"

And then there was the matter
of the broken mirror.
Merely cracked, really.
If the pieces remained in the frame
and he continued to use it
(although his image was a little dicey),
would it make a difference?
About his luck, I mean?

He faced the day as he always did
when the weather was particularly warm
and there were no drafts.
At the heavy glass table,
under a flowering vine fraught with bees,
he ate a yolkless omelet
with dry toast and decaffeinated tea,
spilling salt on his plate in the process,
and throwing a pinch over his left shoulder
into his wife's bowl of Cheerios.

After breakfast, his daughter
wanted them to walk downtown.
As they left the house, he saw
a neighbor's black cat in the street,
so he walked the other direction,
saying to his daughter,
"Let's go this way for a change;
I need the exercise."

His daughter liked to walk on curbs.
He stuck to the sidewalks,
unless they were uneven or broken
or had large cracks in them.
As telephone poles and trees
passed between them,
he would mutter, "Bread and butter"
under his breath.
She looked at him oddly but said nothing.
It was difficult to articulate "B" words
without moving one's lips.

She suddenly ran ahead,
crossed a yard and darted under a ladder.
She waited for him on the sidewalk,
grinning that grin of hers,
suspended in her disbelief
that what she had just done
would have any bearing on her future.

When they arrived home,
his wife suggested
they go for a hike in Muir Woods.
"I've just gone for a walk."
"We only went a few blocks," said his daughter.
"And you do 'need your exercise.'"

This was not going to be a good day.
Looming ahead,
his birthday,
Friday the thirteenth,
and he was out of sick leave.

LEANING

against weathered clapboard siding
under wisteria twisting overhead
in the Indian Summer sun.
The soothing yellow and black hum
of bumblebees is long gone—
deep purple blossoms having given way
to swollen pods hanging.

Through the closed window
CNN expounds upon Trump's
anti-immigrant tweets,
"unrest" in Syria and Hong Kong,
and PG&E shutting off power
to fires they've already started.

I would rather you be leaning
with me
exchanging thoughts
on our daughter's ballet career,
Christo's rolling hills,
or Richard Powers' novel
where trees care for one another.

Instead, I begin to slouch,
not toward Bethlehem,
but in anticipation
of pressure building
in the dangling pods
until they randomly explode.

A Haystack Without a Needle
Is Safer for the Cows

If a stitch in time saves anything,
it better be the whole nine yards.

Unhatched chickens
rolling around whitely
in a red wheelbarrow
are not dependable.
You can't count on them.
I know this to be true
because I got it
from a doctor.

My mother,
the cloud behind
every silver lining,
would have needled
me mercilessly
for voicing this poem aloud
and I would have deserved
a sorrowful licking.

But I will keep on ticking
until those eggs hatch
and the chickens,
white or otherwise,
come home
to roost.

Besides Myself

On the long drive back,
I wondered if I'd make it
to work on time.
And did I really want to be
listening to Pearl Django
imitating the real Reinhardt?

Her thigh

I was thinking about
The croque-monsieurs,
searching for the lost
art of Bonny Doon,
walking the dog,
and souffléd asparagus.

brushed my knee

Missing the CVS no parking sign
had rendered my car
irretrievable:
the towing company was
closed until Monday.

and settled

At an art opening on Thursday,
there was a panel discussion
where an audience member asked,
"If you can't define
what book art is,
why are you here?"

against

CVS will always annoy me,
questions about art will persist,
but all that I've just recalled
pales in comparison
to your touching invitation
and the interwoven reflection on

my thigh

PREFACE TO "SHOOT FIRST"

When I was about twelve years old, I owned a Red Ryder BB gun, and I prided myself in the accuracy with which I hit things. I could shoot a fly off the end of my younger brother's nose... if he had just held still. My mother used to say, "You're going to shoot somebody's eye out with that thing!" I never understood why anyone would *want* their eye shot out. But at that time of my life, I was always mistaking warnings for suggestions.

SHOOT FIRST

A twelve-year-old boy having fun.
It's gone exactly as he planned.
On the ground where he stands is a gun,
and a bird in the palm of his hand.
This does not make him feel like he's won.

Name Dropping

after William Blake's "The Lamb"

I bet he was called Amsterdam.
What else would you call a lamb
but Amsterdam?

You wouldn't call him Pam.
Wrong gender, like Ma'am.
And you wouldn't call him Abram—
too close to Abraham.

Too soft to be called Clam.
Not welcome if he were Scram,
running into things as Wham,
or for that matter, Slam or Bam.

Weighty calling him Kilogram.
I'm not going near Mammogram.
Actually, I don't give a tinker's damn,
make him a vegetable; call him Yam.

Make him king of Siam
or better yet, Buckingham.
But don't strain your diaphragm,
just call him Amsterdam!

In Pursuit of a Kiss

I took your lips for a walk yesterday.
They were pursed against the cold.
Or were they perhaps awaiting a kiss...?
They cantered along beside me
at a regal gait—
they were prancing, really.
(Although, equestrians would call it
a trot.)

Your upper lip was canted
into the wind at an angle
that brought allure to
the fine, fiery fullness
of your lower lip.

Your spirited, unharnessed lips were moving
with such a graceful flair
I couldn't take my eyes off them.
I was so enraptured by their rise and fall
that I trampled wildflowers.
I even failed to notice bystanders
openly gawking at their supple passing.

And when those lustrous red voluptuaries
broke into an imperious gallop,
they suddenly surged ahead of me,
their long, sanguine strides
dimpling into the distance—
not even glancing over their shoulder
as they ended any burgeoning hope.

Country walks are overrated.
Next time, I'll be bolder—
your lips and I will just sit down
with two draft beers,
sip Tomales Bay oysters from their shells,
and add to this quiescent perfection,
an unbridled constancy
of kisses.

GESTATION, PERIOD

There is a noticeable absence of wind in utero,
something those of you already born
might find not worth mentioning.

My mother's belly
could very well be buffeted about—
a ship's sail in a storm,

but I am as snug and provided for
as a queen bee in a honeycomb.
If scientists were to find a way

to extend her gestation period
for the rest of my natural life,
I think I would be quite satisfied.

SLICE

I live in a cottage in the country.
In five years I've had one visitor,
and that person was lost.
So, at the stroke of midnight
one cold winter evening,
I responded with some trepidation
to a knock at my door.

When I opened it,
standing before me
was a tall foreboding figure
with a hooded black cloak
that flowed to the ground.

I said, "Won't you come in?
You look tired and cold."

He seemed a little startled and said,
"Do you know who I am?"

"Well, that long deadly scythe
leaning against my door frame
gives me a clue. Won't you come in
before I catch my death of cold?"

"I'm so used to having the door
slammed in my face.
I'll come in, but I've got to take
you with me when I leave."

I led him to my recliner before the fire
and threw a blanket over his lap.
"You look hungry. Would you like
a nice cup of Japanese tea
with a leftover slice of chocolate cake?"

"A diabetic shouldn't be eating chocolate cake."

"I know, I know, it's bad for my health.
And that's another reason
to offer it to you."

As he sat eating cake and sipping tea,
his hollow gaze wandered around the room
until it landed on a large, framed print
of Albert Pinkham Ryder's *The Race Track*.

He shed his tray and blanket,
walked over to the painting,
and suggestively ran a bony finger
down the rider's pale body.

He said, "That is the best portrait
ever painted of me. I can assure you
those pale slender thighs
gripping the horse's flanks
are incredibly lifelike."

"I'm glad you like it.
I expect you might also admire
those grimly sweeping brush strokes,
the clouded black claw above the horizon,
and the cadaverous fence in the foreground."

"Ryder got it right!
Of the four horses in the Book of Revelation,
the pale one is mine, and Ryder
has us racing toward infinity,
with me as a snake urging myself on."

I thought my guest a little full of himself,
and it was at this moment
I noticed his elevator shoes.
I withheld comment.

"You do know the story
behind Ryder's painting this portrait?"

"Some kid bet all his money
at the track, and when his horse lost,
he shot himself in the head.
Of course I know about it. I was there."

"You would have had to have been there, wouldn't you?
Do you ever wish you led a different kind of existence?"

He savored a bite of cake and took a sip of tea,
pausing to think the question over
before looking up at me with a penetrating gaze
and saying, "What would life on earth
be like without me?

I changed the subject.
"How was your cake and tea?"

"I haven't eaten in years,
so they were both exceptional.
I feel unfamiliar warmth inside.
May I come back and visit
my portrait sometime?"

"You're always welcome,
as a guest,
but what about that scythe
outside my door?"

"Isn't it beautiful?
Even though I use it constantly,
its edge is honed by two swipes
of my butcher's steel.
But no slice of life tonight;
at least not here."

I walked him to the door,
and as I let him out
into the cold night air,
I asked, "Any advice?"

He stared several moments
at the hem of his cloak
before raising his gaunt face
to say, "Lay off the cake,
and maybe stay off Highway 37
the next few weeks."

"And will you be stopping by
the White House anytime soon?"

"I don't take requests!"

And with that, he shouldered his blade,
strode down my narrow path,
and vanished into the dead of night.

SUGAR

When I was a kid
I wanted my eventual death
to occur on top of Hick's Mountain
where the Turkey Vultures
could pick my bones clean—
a view for twenty miles
and no mortuary falderal.

Now, having seen a nature program
with Arctic wolves gnawing
a musk ox carcass,
I think I would be
a sweet dessert for them.

And if I ate a mammoth
bowl of gelato just before
succumbing to their toothy jaws,
would I feel their blood-sugar rise
once eaten?
I would then be part
of a stunning wild beast.

And if one of my wolves were captured
and displaced to Vermont,
to deposit a recently digested meal
under a maple tree,
my sweetness would be
drawn up into the cambium layer
and ultimately bled out
into a bucket,
then distributed in plastic bottles

to be drizzled over
a hefty stack of waffles
and swallowed by a rotund
IHOP regular
dying to become diabetic.

TEARS IN RAIN

Awakened in a dream
as lost as tears in rain
uncertainty at every turn
afraid to breathe

Awakened in a dream
of melancholy rain—
shouldering its weight
sheltering in place

I would rather be
in a floundering lifeboat
with a tiger on board
and no way home

I would rather be
in a punctured raft
on class 5 rapids
my oarsman missing

or feel the pain
in a window's reflection
of an *in-cold-blood* killer
crying raindrops on glass

or face the fear
of drowning
in the plague-infused midst
of everyday life

I would rather be awakened
in any anguished dream
of vulnerability
or impending peril

than to have my psyche
haunted by the smoldering
aura of Kurosawa's
unrelenting rain

Mud-luscious

Rain thrumming on my roof.
It is just spring—early April,
and I pull the covers up
over my pillow
leaving one ear exposed.

It is a soothing sound,
a brook murmuring by.
It is a woman's hand
caressing my shoulder.

I dress and walk outside,
feel my clothes cling
and see the air cleansed
of pollen and corona dust.

I can almost sense
the poppy seeds I planted
winging their way to the surface
to burst into air
and become neighbors—
red and gold invitations
to the beleaguered honeybee.

Standing there
soaking up California rain,
I am reminded of my daughter
running out into a downpour
to pick mangoes in Maui,
her two cousins and their mother
yelling from the doorway,
"Come in before you catch cold."

A contrarian, my daughter
rolls down a soggy slope
in her pajamas
because it is mud-luscious
and 82 degrees.

TAKE 5

It's a kind of blue 1959—
and Miles to go before we sleep.
Coltrane's taking giant steps
when suddenly Brubeck's
pollywogs are on the loose.

Time for six-four, three-four,
nine-eight, and five-four.
Not Columbia's thing—
time out until '61.

Take Five added—
two takes to record
what Desmond called
a last-minute throwaway.

But Brubeck's vamp
under Morello's solo
made me cross that bridge,
roll up the living room,
and dance a blue rondo
across the rug-free floor.

The tune picks up,
sticks with me
like the strange meadow lark's song
from my childhood.

Brubeck calls one chord progression,
"Oom, junka, junk, boom, boom.
Oom, junka, junk," and one theme,
"Dopa, depa, depa, dopa,
lom, bom, bom, bom."

It all boils down to this:

LET'S

after Prartho Sereno

Let's hang sheets of rain on a clothesline,
dangle lavender bundles from curtain rods,
carry bars of soap in our pockets
to scrub the stricken air.

Let's pull up weeds and plant them
in places they won't recognize.

Bring hummingbirds inside
to hover in our living rooms.

Let beetles burrow through memories
to get to the bottom of things.

Our minds are too much on hold.

Let's free them to slip
by that ominous cloud,

and patchwork a quilt
of front porch stories
that make no sense
to the fearful heart.

Elanus

A White-tailed Kite, poetry in flight,
hovering in place with falcating wings
resisting the pull of the big blue.

From his perch on air
he can spot moving prey
a mile away.

He makes an easy target
for any young boy with a gun
in a hurry to prove himself.

Bicycling home from Bodega Bay,
I find one kid's proof
on a barbed-wire fence.

Still alive, left wing hanging.
I wrap him in a towel,
nestle him into my backpack,

pedal to the vet's.
Shoulder joint shattered—
nothing to be done.

I take him home,
force feed him ground meat
for three days.

Up close,
eyes of explosive amber,
wreathed in black.

Black shoulder patches
on grey wings
that won't feel flight again.

From the ground looking up,
the bird is all white.
Elanus leucurus majusculus,

endangered for posing on air.
I bury him where
the only thing above him

is the sky he once owned.

BUG

Took my father's flashlight
to crawl under the house.

About twenty feet in,
came face to face
with a bug the size
of a waffle iron.

Gladiator's armored body,
legs everywhere,
opposable claws
at their ends.
Beady masked eyes sunk
in a huge copper head—
bludgeon-shaped.
Jaws that could strip
a body clean in an hour.

It hissed and spat
the odor of vomit,
its mouth expanding
in four directions—
fangs all around.
Became a question
of who could crawl
faster.

Before going to bed that night,
I tucked the covers in tight.
The bug got under them.

When I woke up,
flesh was missing
from my right leg,
and my mother was yelling
through the door,
"Get dressed
or you'll be late for school!
And take that ugly bug
with you!"

Even my own
personal monster
should be free
to crawl in the dirt
looking for potatoes.

As my mother said,
"The bugs you've got
to worry about
are the ones you can't see."

VISION

The dark-haired girl
hastening toward me,
weaving through startled male glances
amid Market Street hustle.
A starburst being recognized—
an ephemera fleeing my gaze.

It was her look of concern that got me.
Twenty seconds of a sky-blue dress
with shimmering white polka dots—
a girl leaving astonishment in her wake.

She had the aura of a Renoir
in an uncharacteristic hurry.
A seed in my memory bank
still bearing fruit.
No reason.
No reason at all.

If

If your train of thought
happened to be caught
rippling across
the smooth stones of the Yuba,
would the sound be the same?

And if that resonant river
had beneath its chromatic
surface, rainbow trout
thirsting for caddisflies,
would the big one laugh at your lure?

If you decided instead
to go for a swim
in a deep green pool
with the stream ambling through it,
would the fish really care?

And as you walked
through the woods,
would the evergreen air
displace the exhaust
of the life you left behind?

If we could be there again—
a gathering of friends
yielding hats to the wind,
forming bridges across the water
with a symphonic wandering of words,

we could then wend our way home.

GRAVITY

Those for whom gravity
is greater than desire,
have wings too frail to keep
their incendiary bodies
above the flames.

A lantern burns brightly
on a grassy knoll
until it runs out of oil,
leaving the moths unfulfilled.

Unable to resist
his fervent will to do good,
a moonlighting library tech
hand-delivers a newspaper
and gets run over by his car.

A teenage boy has
a Blue Moon Mambo
with a Black Lagoon woman
of a certain age,
who leaves his ashes behind.

Rise above the earthbound.
Ignite your impassioned tinder
and achieve a personal zenith.
If gravity pulls you into flames,
what a lovely way to burn.

A MOMENT

I am exiting a restaurant on a narrow cobblestone street in the Tuscan village of Poppi. I look to my right and see Joel and Eliana already ahead of me, walking toward the arched stone entrance to the village. Joel's jacket from this morning is around his waist. He is carrying Eliana's backpack for her and his right hand is resting lightly on her blue and white striped shirt, just below the nape of her neck. I am too far behind them to hear what they may be saying to one another. In fact, by the attitude of their heads, it doesn't appear they are talking.

It doesn't matter. I am watching a moment in time that makes me inexplicably happy. They are silhouetted against a long unbroken facade of buildings, earthen yellow in the late afternoon sun. They are just in each other's company, walking—my friend of 35 years and my 16-year-old daughter.

Moments like this should be etched in stone.

Salutations

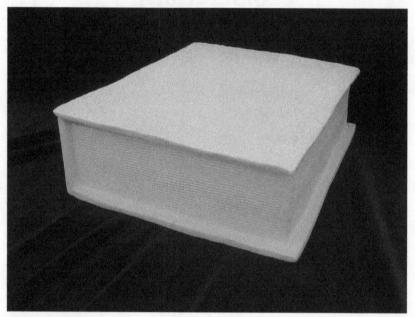

Before the Beep
Porcelain Book
7 X 9 X 2.5 inches.

PREFACE TO *BEFORE THE BEEP*

For years now, I have recorded greetings on my answering machine or voice mail, and for my birthday a couple of years ago, my daughter transcribed her favorites into a book she bound herself. And so, I decided to do the same, only with a nod toward fragile clay tablets, copper telephone lines, the printed word, and other evanescent modes of expression.

Before the Beep is a porcelain book I made to house alternatives to the prerecorded greetings we have grown all too accustomed to hearing when someone is unavailable to answer our calls. I wanted this sculpture to be a reminder of the incredible span of the written word—from Bronze Age clay tablets to the dizzying developments of today's technology. These invitations to leave a message "after the beep" provide glimpses into the crooked meanderings of my mind and, for some of you, perhaps, a moment of reflection or, in some cases, a stunned spasm of bewilderment.

Before the Beep

The fact that no one understands you doesn't mean you're an artist. I am, however, looking forward to being refreshed and challenged by your unique point of view, after the beep.

If one were to drop a golf ball from a great height onto the belly of a peacefully sleeping cat, one could not expect to avoid comment. As the ringing of my telephone sometimes has a similar effect on me, thank you for calling when I am not here to feel its impact.

As I rode my new bike for the first time yesterday, I deftly dodged an old lady doddering along the sidewalk and experienced a small boy's notion of having done good. Please leave an artful dodge of your own, after the beep.

Neither sure-footed nor clear, I am out on a leafless limb with just spider webs and moss, listening to the silken slip of water over stone. After the beep, please leave a not too jarring earful that will suspend nothing more than my solitude.

Your message will probably not send a flurry of palpitations through the Gallery of Important Things Said, but leave it after the beep anyway, as my expectations are unreasonably high.

Sometimes I forget to press "Listen," and I carry around my negligence like a bowling ball, for the rest of the day envisioning your message just lying there, a fallen tree in the forest, soundlessly waiting.

What you are about to say may have nothing to do with love, but, after the beep, begin, and we'll see.

A moment ago, I dimmed the light and looked down at her face as it leaned into linen shadows, and I thought for a moment Latour had painted this soft luminescence. Please forgive my reluctance to answer the phone.

After the beep, please speak up; I need to hear the petals hit the ground.

As I am rowing upstream, Ophelia floats by and I become caught in the billows of her dress and am borne downstream, trailing after her against my better judgment. There seems to be a message here. After the beep, I hear *your* voice.

Leave the vast calamity of my existence unknown to me. After the beep, speak only of ripe nectarines and happiness fully endowed, or I shall remain as reticent as stones in a stream, resisting the burbling flow.

If this is the mime troupe returning my call, on second thought, send me a letter. All others may talk at length on matters of interest to me. Otherwise, please leave me a pantomimed message, after the beep.

I'd like your message to give me a sudden inhalation of joy—a reflexive gasp of awe and wonder—like seeing a Ferris wheel for the first time. Of course, if, after the beep, you fall a little short of this expectation, my response may lack the warmth and vigor you might otherwise have received.

After the beep, please sow a few palliative seeds in the consumptive orchard of my mind.

It's not raining today and I am leaning against the siding of this old house with a book in my hand, basking in the silky warmth of early spring sunlight on my face, while in your hand you hold a phone, waiting for the beep.

If you are calling because I failed to return your call, it is because your words, at some point, simply stumbled into the black hole of my memory. This message will repeat.

As muddled messages are often more intriguing than those of perfect clarity, please leave something easily misinterpreted, after the beep.

After the beep, please leave a sonnet extolling my virtues. If you feel you can't lie, make something up.

When I enter a room full of books, I move slowly among them as their spines announce the intrigues held within. I could pull one down and pry it open, but that would be too familiar an act. After the beep, please voice an impropriety of your own.

Never lend a friend a book. They seldom come back. I know this from experience; half the books I own have been lent to me—but not, of course, by you.

Today is a good day to eat something that makes your taste buds drool at the very thought of it: summer berry pudding, Zuni chicken, three berry mint custard tart, or my grandmother's huckleberry pie. Then, after the beep, give me a vicarious thrill.

Spring is Point Reyes wildflowers, goslings at Shollenberger, bumblebees in the wisteria, and Linda's perfectly random garden. If this isn't the answer to your question, say what you meant to say, after the beep.

I would have answered the phone, just now, if I weren't knee-deep in lethargy. After the beep, leave me a few of your virtues and I will prioritize my calls later.

Lint filters always end up with more lint in them than was on the clothes, and my lint filter is leaking. Please be kind; after the beep, make sure the message you are about to leave, leaves any loose threads of thought, dusty ideas, and clinging particles of wisdom behind.

The immediate joy inherent in the act of speaking with me will be lost by tossing words into this uncaring machine. But if you feel you must, toss away, after the beep.

After the beep, deposit your words in this machine. Someday there may be some unforeseen need for them.

Your message is unclear to me, as I am not here to hear it, and when I am here, I am likely to be sitting on the back steps watching the violets bloom along the broken tile path. Please say something that doesn't require my immediate attention, after the beep.

I should be here to answer your call, but I am off somewhere at Point Reyes dreaming of huckleberries and the pies they will become. After the beep, please let me know the practicalities of what I am missing.

My yard could use less weeds and more seeds. It's just-spring—leave me your mud-luscious vision, even if it too is a bit muddled, after the beep.

A politician's thoughts often clog as if a comb working stiffly through his mind has struck a snarl. Please try to keep your stream of consciousness flowing, after the beep.

I have been told I am descended from a long line my mother once listened to. Leave me a line, after the beep, and I'll get back to you on how effective it was.

Sonny Rollins blows long and he blows hard and he always has a tinge of excitement. Blow your own horn loudly after the beep. If you do it well, I will forgive your noise.

My mother used to say to me: "*Te vendam si non bene (CIX) moratus es.*" ["I'll sell you if you don't behave."] Unfortunately, there were no buyers. If you have any latent interest, please express it after the beep. *Veni, Vidi, vendidi.* ["I came, I saw, I sold out."]

If you're an eschatologist, you may want to ask about the unopened packet of rice crackers, the salami, the kiwifruit marmalade jar, and the sachet of no brand dehydrated noodles at the back of the bottom shelf. If not, just leave your regular message, after the beep.

In wishing to disturb the serene tranquility in which my cat and I live, before you speak, consider the danger in which you place yourself. Of course, there exists the possibility your message will bring me happiness, and since you risk so little, I shall offer you a beep.

Were I able to answer the phone right now, I would be inserting a bookmark into the heretofore undiminished momentum of my day. So, after the beep, please leave me a few of the perplexing intricacies of your day as it rushes toward completion.

This may not be a form of optimism with which you are familiar, but I am, at the moment, recovering from the message you are about leave, after the beep.

After the beep, please leave me a Chopin nocturne or a Miles Davis sketch. Of course, the melodic tone of your voice will do, especially if you impart something I am anxious to hear.

As you are the crème of all brûlées, leave a little somethin' somethin' after the beep.

At this moment, I am only one finger extended through a chain-link fence in the hopes of running it slowly down a dust-brown horse's velvet nose. Perhaps, after the beep, you could extend me this courtesy.

I have just been given a three-month-old kitten, who I have named Misha because he leaps with the unerring grace of Baryshnikov. After the beep, please leave a message that dances through my receiver.

Pablo Neruda once asked why trees concealed the splendor of their roots. After the beep, please reveal a hidden treasure of your own.

You are about to leave your name and phone number, for without your unbridled assistance, I would have given up trying to recognize you in the surging wave of the next moment.

The artist Chuck Close once said, "Inspiration is for amateurs; the rest of us just get to work." After the beep, please leave an inspirational message that will help me ascend to the level of rank amateur.

Words can become a living thing when they move the astonished air to sing. Beethoven's inner ear was attuned to such music. I am a metaphor for is—I live to make art and die at its completion. Leave something of your own making, after the beep.

Before I run headlong into the words you are about to leave, I am going to try to remember the last time I sat in a swing, with someone behind me, joyfully pushing.

My answering machine is limited. Should I not already know you, please leave a clear impression after the beep. I feel grace in the offing.

When lilacs last in the dooryard bloomed, I was sitting on the staircase awaiting your call.

Hold your message until it has grown heavy in your mind, then release it to dangle at my end of the line until I can pluck it, like a ripe pear, after the beep.

STEVE TRENAM

There are few activities that give me more pleasure than nudging words across the blankly disquieting page, and pushing clay around, into, and through itself. I have been fortunate to work in two disciplines, writing and ceramics, and I have discovered the end result seldom exactly matches the goal in either. It is the work that matters—the engagement of my imagination, the intuitive use of my mind and hands. In the end, the artist discovers art has a mind of its own, and it is these repeated realizations that enrich my life. As much as any other work that I do, these small transformative journeys carry me (for the most part) forward.

My mother owned a bookstore from 1962 to 1985 in Petaluma, California. It was called Alta's Old Book Shop, and its value lay not in glossy modernity, but in its being a sort of dusty delivery room for the birth of ideas. It was for me, a refuge from hasty judgment, a source for answers and insights which enlarged my personal life and gave it meaning, and also generated an impulse to write.

I am currently teaching a poetry writing class at the Vintage House Senior Center in Sonoma as part of the Santa Rosa Junior College Older Adults Program. There is magic in this group of people; they are blossoming as poets and contributing immeasurably to my own ability to write poetry. I am most thankful for their presence in my life.

CPSIA information can be obtained
at www.ICGtesting.com
Printed in the USA
FSHW010705291020
75257FS